STAY ON THE PATH, DUMB-ASS

What is Thinking – Visual Aspirations to Self-Help

by

Michael B. Hamilton

PITTSBURGH, PENNSYLVANIA 15222

The contents of this work including, but not limited to, the accuracy of events, people, and places depicted; opinions expressed; permission to use previously published materials included; and any advice given or actions advocated are solely the responsibility of the author, who assumes all liability for said work and indemnifies the publisher against any claims stemming from publication of the work.

All Rights Reserved
Copyright © 2010 by Michael B. Hamilton
No part of this book may be reproduced or transmitted in any form or by any means, electronic or mechanical, including photocopying, recording, or by any information storage and retrieval system without permission in writing from the author.

ISBN: 978-1-4349-9694-7
Printed in the United States of America

First Printing

For more information or to order additional books,
please contact:
RoseDog Books
701 Smithfield Street
Pittsburgh, Pennsylvania 15222
U.S.A.
1-800-834-1803
www.rosedogbookstore.com

WHAT I
DO WITH
TODAY
BECOMES
MY
TOMORROW
!¡!

IN EVERY WORLD, AND IN EVERY WAY THE FUTURE IS ALWAYS A BECOMING !¡!

I AM THE KEEPER Of MY OWN DESTINEY, I WAIK THE PATH I CHOOSE !i!

TODAY IS THE BEST DAY OF MY LIFE SIMPLY BECAUSE I HAVE SEEN IT !¡!

WE
ALL HAVE
THE
POTENTIAL
TO
SUCCEED
!¡!

THE HARDEST
PART OF
CHANGE, IS
LEARNING
THAT YOU
CAN
!¡!

SHAPE
YOUR
FUTURE
BECOME
YOUR
DESTINY
!¡!

YOU
ONLY
REJECT
YOURSELF
BY NOT
TRYING
!¡!

WHAT
IS
CHOICE
WHEN
YOU HAVE
CHOSEN
!¡!

IT
IS
MY
CHOICE
TOO
!¡!

THE KEY TO
HAPPINESS
LIVES IN
THE WHO
YOU CAN
BECOME
!¡!

IF NEVER
WAS
FOREVER,
THEN FOREVER
COUID
NEVER
BE !¡!

MIRACLES
HAPPEN
WHEN THEY
BEGIN
WITH
PLEASE
!¡!

BE
THE
BELIEVER
IN
YOU
!¡!

I
AM
A
GROWING
INSPIRATION
!¡!

GET
DIRECTION
THEN
DETERMINE
YOUR
DISPOSITION
!¡!

I'M
O.K.
TOO
GROW
!¡!

YOU
ARE THE
BEST
PART OF
TODAY'S
MIRACLE
!¡!

TOGETHER
WE
CAN
ME
MYSELF
AND I
!¡!

A
POSITIVE
ROUTINE
GOES A
LONG
WAY
!¡!

STRENGTH
IS
PROVEN
IN
ADVESITY
!¡!

EVERYDAY

ENDS

WITH A

MIRACLE

!¡!

DISCOVER
YOUR
ABILITIES
INFLUENCE
YOUR
TALENTS
!¡!

MAKE A
GOOD SPOT
AND
HELP IT
GROW
!¡!

BUILD
WHERE
YOU
WISH
TO
SUCCEED
!¡!

PASSION
IS
HALF
THE
FACE OF
COURAGE
!¡!

I CAN

I CAN

I

CAN

!¡!

WHEN I
RODE WITH
NEGATIVE
NEGATIVE
DROVE
ME
!¡!

THOSE THAT CAN'T, WILL ALWAYS TELL YOU – YOU CAN'T BECAUSE YOU CAN !¡!

LIFE IS TO
EXPERIENCE
LEARN
REALIZE
EMBRACE
BALANCE
ACHIEVE
AND
BECOME !¡!

FATHER I BELIEVE

If I fade away in the quiet distance, then I am just another sand in time, I leave a piece of me here and there, for in every memory, there lives a sie. Now I don't know where I'm gonna go, or even who's eyes I might see, but I remember the times I share with each, and all the feelings they leave in me, so I hold my head up high in the sky, yet I can't always stay off my knees, for I feel every tear that runs down both cheeks, when I'm screaming, "Father I Believe," but still I ride on the winds beneath my wings, and still I try, always hoping for my dreams, but that's my drive – to climb my hill of destiny, because I don't know what tomorrow brings, All I know — I'm nothing more than me!¡!

"The greatest part of family lives within a touch!¡!"

Mom, Dad, James, Bre, Terri, John, Bev, Brice, Renee, Kim, Chad, Forest, Leah, Stan, Theresa, Pat, Jonny-T!¡!

– Rock the Universe –

Michael Hamilto

#14